Spiritual

Pupils as Leaders of Collective Worship

Rebecca Swansbury
Deputy Director of Education, Diocese of Canterbury

GROVE BOOKS LIMITED
RIDLEY HALL RD CAMBRIDGE CB3 9HU

Contents

Acknowledgments

This book is dedicated to all the young people I had the privilege of meeting during my research. I am grateful to all the school staff who facilitated these conversations and shared their experience with me. Thank you to Ian Terry and Alison Farnell for their supervision and encouragement, and to my wonderful colleagues and family who have supported me throughout this journey. Natalie, your prophetic input shaped the direction of this book; thank you for hearing and responding to God's gentle nudge.

First Impression October 2024
ISSN 2041-0964
ISBN 978 1 78827 421 0

A Vision of What Could Be

1

Four slightly nervous Year 5 pupils stand at the front of the hall, as the rest of the school community dance into the space to an upbeat worship song. The candle is lit, the usual greeting liturgy is shared and the pupil leaders spring to life. The once anxious pupils confidently step forward to share their planned act of worship. The message is simply communicated through a dramatic reading of a Bible story, followed by real-life illustrations. Then comes the most powerful part. The pupils change the mood in the hall, from laughter and observation, to a time of personal spiritual reflection. They pose deeply thought-provoking questions about the characters within the story. They hold the space. By lingering longer, they allow all to ponder in the quiet. Their childlike curiosity and freedom enables pupils to ask questions that dig into the meaning of the story in a way I have not seen adults do before. When all are invited to pray, you can sense a spiritual connection to the words being said, as all have an opportunity to consider their place in the story.

In this school, pupil-led worship was part of the regular rhythm of collective worship. The young people had an equal role with the staff in the planning and leading of daily worship. They were trusted to do so. When asked, other pupils said their favourite acts of worship were those led by pupils, as they could connect with what they were saying in a deeper way. This empowering school culture allowed the young people to flourish as worship leaders. It did not happen overnight; the culture of trust was established gradually, enabling everyone to be more attentive to each other and to God. Indeed, Robert Coles has suggested that if adults waited attentively and listened to children, they too could realize that they were children of God.[1] And so, everyone in the school community might develop together.

A Journey

This journey began for me in 2016 when I began training Religious Education (RE) leaders in Canterbury diocesan schools to use the resource *Understanding Christianity*. Inevitably, staff and pupils were going to be challenged to think more deeply, learn to critically analyze biblical texts and explore theological concepts.

As I began this work in schools, my thoughts turned to collective worship and the experiences pupils had within it. Young people would soon be analyzing biblical texts using a hermeneutical approach in RE, yet in collective worship they were often told what the message of worship or a Bible story was. If young people could ask and respond to challenging questions about the biblical text they were exploring in RE, why could there not be a similar expectation in collective worship?

More questions emerged. Could collective worship provide a safe space for young people to question, wonder and reflect on what they were hearing, without being told, 'The meaning of this story is…'? Could the voice of young people, their views and interpretations, be included and form a regular part of worship? What might a school culture look like where this was the reality and the norm? Could this be created authentically and become the everyday rhythm of worship?

The Place of Collective Worship in the School System

Before we explore that journey towards transforming collective worship through the leadership of pupils, it is important to clarify what is meant by 'collective worship.' The Education Reform Act 1988, and guidance contained within the DfE circular *1/94* (1994), seeks to define what collective worship is, whilst setting out the legal obligations and parameters for school leaders.[2] Paragraph 57 of the circular explains that collective worship should be special, set apart from other school activities and offer reverence to the divine.

Collective worship must also differ from corporate worship, where believers gather to deepen their faith, such as Christians gathering for worship in church. Collective worship in school must make no assumption as to the personal faith of those participating. Through invitational language, it can be inclusive of all faiths and none. This is explained in the guidance document for collective worship in Church of England schools:

> Worship should be truly welcoming, inclusive and exemplifying the principles of Christian hospitality. This is an approach that seeks to meet the needs of all, wherever they may be on their journey of faith and belief.[3]

The acts of worship I will be writing about will be reflective of the Church of England guidance and parameters of the DfE circular and illustrate why collective worship should be contextually appropriate.

The Why

Having a clear, school-specific vision as to why you want to develop pupils as collective worship leaders should be behind any decision to do so. Maybe that is why you are reading this book. You need to consider how pupils leading worship will enhance the spiritual flourishing both of the pupil leaders and those pupils and adults present in worship.

Many school leaders have been led to believe that pupil leadership is an obligation in church school collective worship. However, as noted in the 2022–2023 National SIAMS (Statutory Inspection of Anglican and Methodist Schools) Report:

> Schools would benefit from being empowered to make contextually-appropriate decisions on this issue, including a consideration of whether, and how, leadership of worship universally enhances pupils' and adults' spiritual flourishing. They should then make decisions accordingly.[4]

Therefore, school leaders should not feel compelled to put together a group of pupil leaders for collective worship just because others have.

In sharing my passion for the intrinsic role I believe pupils play in the worshipping life of the school, my 'why' is to:

- Empower school leaders to trust and include the voice of pupils;
- Give permission to leaders to allow pupils space to grow as worship leaders, in a culture where they feel safe to take risks and make mistakes;
- Reassure leaders that developing a pupil worship leader group is not about ticking a box, fulfilling criteria for an inspection or following the latest education fad;
- Remind leaders that nurturing pupil worship leaders reflects a desire to empower them to share their voice so that all those within worship hear them.

Your 'why' may be different and that is OK. Each context is unique; young people leading worship will look different in each school. Start with your 'why,' be clear about your purpose and this will direct and determine the 'what' and the 'how.'

The subsequent chapters describe anecdotally how young people, whatever their age, faith or cultural background, can authentically lead worship which is appropriate for their community. Drawing upon good practice from across a number of Anglican dioceses and examples from Scripture, we will consider the place of young people as worship leaders and the role adults play in facilitating this.

2 Children as Spiritual Agents

Alfred Pang refers to children as being spiritual agents of God's presence.[5] Being an agent conjures up an image of an active person undertaking a mission to bring about change. Children as spiritual agents is a powerful image of how children can actively bring spiritual change and formation to their lives and the lives of others. Humans are born spiritual beings. Just as young babies grow and develop with age, the same can be said for their spiritual capacity. Children may not have the spiritual language or reflective understanding of an adult, but their open, curious and holistic view of the world makes living spiritually far easier for children than adults. Theologian Karl Rahner, writing in 1963, said, 'Children are finite human beings with an infinite openness to God as mystery.'[6]

Rebecca Nye's research builds on this by describing children's spirituality as, 'an initially natural capacity for awareness of the sacred quality to life experiences.'[7]

This positive view of children as spiritual beings has not always been the case. Writing in 1964, Ronald Goldman took a view that

> mystics, who claim to have direct sensations of the divine, are exceptions, but…they are extremely rare cases, rarer in adolescence and practically unknown in childhood.[8]

This claim supported the view of many adults, that children were spiritually empty and only when an adult intervened would grow spiritually. Other metaphors like 'blank slates ready to be written on,' 'sponges ready to soak up knowledge' or 'wet clay to be moulded' further embedded this. The passive nature of these images shaped how adults behaved towards children. Spiritual formation was seen as something that was done *to* children.

Rebecca Nye and David Hay, through their research, disputed Goldman's claims:

> The mistake he made was to assume that spiritual awareness is always something extraordinary, equated with mystic ecstasy, instead of holding open the possibility that it might be a very ordinary aspect of young children's everyday experience.[9]

More recently, however, there has been a shift in thinking about the spiritual capabilities and formation of children. They are now often described as 'pilgrims,' 'plants' or 'sheep.' These metaphors describe how adults walk *with* children, acting as a shepherd or farmer, helping them grow and develop their spirituality. Sociologist David Oswell explains that children's spiritual agency should not be seen as something they have or do not have, and set apart from the world of adults. He goes on to say that:

> Children's spiritual agency is lived out in the intersection of our lives… and is discerned in the difference children could make in transforming the faith of adults.[10]

Therefore children, as spiritual beings, have a valid and important voice to share. What might happen if we, as adults, do not provide space or opportunities for children to develop their own spiritual language and understanding?

Biblical Spiritual Agents

> Paying heed to the spiritual agency of children is respecting the dignity that lies at the heart of being in a just relationship with them.[11]

Spiritual agents who are also young people ripple through the Bible narrative. The spiritual nature of children and their ability to bring positive change to a situation is an integral part of God's plan for humanity:

> Through the praise of children and infants you have established a stronghold against your enemies, to silence the foe and the avenger. (Ps 8.2; NIV)

Where some might view children as insignificant, or weak, God makes it abundantly clear that children have a mighty role to play in his kingdom. Usually, the breaking of strongholds and silencing enemies would not be associated with the work of children. Yet King David, the writer of this psalm, recognizes that the voice of young children carries divine strength and power. How often do we ask children to join with others in prayer, or ask them to speak directly into situations?

There are many occasions in the Old Testament where God used young people to speak directly into situations. Joseph, Josiah, Miriam, Esther, David and Daniel were likely all to be teenagers or young adults when God called them to serve him. Their significant messages to God's people brought hope and freedom, alongside calls to repentance and the changing of their ways. God clearly valued and trusted the voices of children and young people.

God's trust in young people can be seen when Mary, a young teenager, was given the highest honour of carrying Jesus, God's son:

> But the angel said to her, 'Do not be afraid, Mary, you have found favour with God. You will conceive and give birth to a son, and you are to call him Jesus. (Luke 1.30–31, NIV)

Mary, as a young woman, from a humble family and unmarried at the time, would have been the last person chosen by polite society to carry the Son of God. This intentional choice demonstrated God's love for those marginalized by society. By being obedient and open to God's call, Mary became a spiritual agent, transforming lives through her actions and faith.

The gospel writers included many accounts of Jesus going out of his way to interact with children who were suffering physically or spiritually. In a time when the young were seen as insignificant, it is clear children were important to Jesus and his time with them was not wasted. He rebuked the disciples for turning infants away (Mark 10.13–16), attended the bedside of a young girl who had died (Mark 5.21–24, 35–43), used the lunch of a young boy to feed thousands (John 6.9) and cast out demons from a young Greek girl (Mark 7.26, 30). Jesus' high regard for, and value placed on, children obviously impacted those around him, hence the inclusion of these accounts in the gospel narratives.

The quickly expanding early Christian church mirrored Jesus' view that children and young people were a vital part of the community. Those who began to spread the gospel message had young apprentices. They would be developed as leaders before eventually being sent out on their own. One of these apprentices was Timothy. He followed and learnt from the apostle Paul. In his letter to Timothy, Paul encourages him to keep going and not to be discouraged by those who think he is too young to serve or minister to others:

> Don't let anyone look down on you because you are young, but set an example for the believers in speech, in conduct, in love, in faith and in purity. (1 Tim 4.12, NIV)

How can we encourage our young people to speak out in truth and inspire others to live a life shaped by morality and love?

The Role of Adults in Enabling Children and Young People to be Spiritual Agents

Let us not deceive ourselves. Having emphasized how important it is to listen to children, we could assume that this is the only role played by adults. By no means! Carefully trained adults must teach children how to ask productive questions, and how to think in curious and inquisitive ways. Mark Chater, in his book *Jesus Christ, Learner Teacher,* describes how, as a child, he was grateful that the adults who surrounded him gave him substantial theology yet held back from trying to tell him everything.[12] We want to teach children how to think, not what to think. Too often in worship the adults think they have the only answer, so proceed to tell those listening how to understand the Bible story being explored. Through this practice, many children may feel that their thoughts must be wrong if they do not match up with the answers given by the adults.

Instead, one can use open, wondering questions, like, 'I wonder what you think this passage means?' or, 'I wonder why Jesus told this story?' These open questions allow, and invite, all to consider for themselves what the meaning might be. Mark Chater continues his childhood story:

> On the whole, they avoided the twin mistakes of condescension—making it too simple, too nice, too child centred—and over-explanation—attempting to explain, qualify every ritual act and puzzling text.[13]

Teaching young people how to think and wonder will create deeper, more personal meanings for each of them. In turn, this facilitates their growing as effective spiritual agents who are capable of ministry *to* those they are serving.

Reflecting on the *Faith in the Nexus* research, Trevor Cooling concludes:

> The Nexus research seems to be saying that the oft-made assumption that the adult role is to provide correct answers for children's faith questions is ill-conceived. Rather we should respect children's spiritual leadership and give more emphasis to engaging in exploratory conversations and sharing in faith-nurturing practices with them.[14]

Church schools can encourage pupils to be attentive to God as well as to each other. One of the clearest biblical instances of this attentiveness in action is in the story of the boy, Samuel, and the elderly priest, Eli:

> So Eli told Samuel, 'Go and lie down, and if he calls you, say, "Speak, Lord, for your servant is listening."' So Samuel went and lay down in his place. The Lord came and stood there, calling as at the other times, 'Samuel! Samuel!' Then Samuel said, 'Speak, for your servant is listening.' (1 Sam 3.9–10, NIV)

Observe how Eli responded to Samuel. In a time when the word of the Lord was rare (1 Sam 3.1), Eli was wise enough to recognize that God could be speaking to Samuel, despite his young age. So, rather than getting in the way of Samuel's interaction with God, Eli stood to the side, making space for Samuel to listen. I wonder how you might have responded in this situation?

In Jesus' times, a rabbi's apprentices were told to stay close to their rabbi, so as to learn everything from them through observation and imitation. By staying so close they would often end up covered in the dust kicked up by the rabbi's feet![15]

Questions to Consider

- How close do we allow our pupil leaders to get to adults who plan and lead worship? Do we allow them to hear and see the thought and planning process that goes into creating an act of worship?
- Do we create opportunities for pupils to observe worship and take notes on how questions are asked and responded to, or question the language used to invite the community to pray for example? How 'dusty' are our pupil worship leaders?
- How dust-covered are we as adults as we learn from the pupils who plan, lead and evaluate acts of worship?

In summary, Nye sets this challenge:

> We often tell a Bible story, but rather than trusting God's word to speak for itself in God's own way, we rush to explain what it says to us. We miss the chance to explore how it can make meaning for the child.[16]

Enabling and empowering spiritual children to be spiritual agents is not as hard as adults may think. By stepping back like Eli and trusting the voice of the child, we can guide our children to notice, wonder and respond as spiritual agents.

Gennesaret—A Land Where Diverse Plants Flourish Together

3

The largest faith group represented in our school is Muslim. Therefore, the way we plan and lead worship has to ensure every pupil knows they belong and feels part of the act of worship. We have built relationships with the Imam and parents so they can advise and articulate what their children can be part of and do within worship. Over time, we have cultivated a trusting, open, worshipping community where all our children, Muslim, Christian, Hindu and those of no faith, join side by side for worship every day. Our shared spirituality is what unites us. Each day, worship provides a safe, deeply spiritual space that celebrates faith. This allows all to respect one another and express and enact their beliefs openly.

Head teacher of a Church of England primary school

Gennesaret

Gennesaret is the Hebrew name given to a piece of land about three or four miles long on the western border of the Sea of Galilee, in Israel. Jesus was very familiar with this area as it was well known for its incredibly fertile soils. This was due to its geographical location and plentiful water supplies. Jesus often spent time in and around there. It was where Jesus met and called the first disciples (Luke 5.1-11), where the disciples anchored the boat after Jesus had calmed the storm (Mark 6.53) and where Jesus healed the sick (Matt 14.34–35). Writers at the time of Jesus, and since, described the fertility of the Gennesaret soils and the beauty of its rich ecosystem. Different and unexpected fruits and plants flourished alongside each other in the rich soil, benefitting from its microclimate. It is said that walnut, palm, olive and fig trees flourished together in this place, trees that do not usually grow in the same soil.

Questions to Consider

- What strikes you about this place?
- What does this illustration make you think about in the context of collective worship in our increasingly diverse school communities?
- Does your school 'soil' enable all to flourish in faith, within their own integrity, like the ancient trees in Gennesaret?

The Walnut, the Palm, the Olive and the Fig Tree Flourish Together Here

When thinking about our schools, what might a place where the 'walnut, palm, olive and fig tree flourish together' look like in reality? In *Our Hope for a Flourishing Future,* the Church of England Education Office (CEEO) share their vision for a school that embraces all:

> A vision for education centred on dignity and respect enables flourishing children to learn from, and grow alongside, others who are different from themselves in good schools which celebrate equity, diversity, belonging, inclusion and justice at every opportunity.[17]

Creating a diverse community built on welcome and inclusion of all authentically embodies the example Jesus set to his followers. Diversity is something to cherish and celebrate, not fear.

> For me, the inclusive nature of church schools is why, as a person of Jewish faith, I choose to lead a school where diverse faith communities learn and work together. It is vital that our children learn about tolerance, one another's beliefs and practices, and the importance of respecting opinions and thoughts that are different to their own. This wouldn't happen if the school was monocultural. By welcoming and including everyone together in one school, we flourish and grow in our appreciation and understanding of each other.
>
> Executive head teacher, Church of England infant school

Through developing long-term trusting relationships, many church school leaders have cultivated school communities that truly embrace diversity.

How Can We Draw Upon the Wisdom of Our School Leaders in Bringing Together Diverse Faith and Belief Traditions Within an Act of Distinctively Christian Worship?

This is what some of them say:

> *Time*—It takes time to build trusting relationships with families. Do not rush this. Take them with you on each step of the journey. Include families in decisions and discussions. Get to know them and listen attentively, so that you really understand what their issues might be. This will allow you to work together to address them.

Clear communication—From the outset, be open and honest with parents about who you are as a Church of England school. Allow them space to ask you questions. Be clear that worship is not about indoctrination but invitation. Share the school's Christian vision and values. Invite families to discuss how these connect with their own faith tradition.

Have an open door—Invite parents into the school to join for worship. Narrate each element, so they can see why each happens and what is expected. Allow parents to see how the children are respected and included in worship. Demonstrate how they are invited to pray, sing and reflect. Model how space is created for each child, within their own faith, to grow spiritually through worship.

Build relationships with those who lead, or who are part of, the faith communities locally. Use their wisdom to guide you in making decisions around the planning of worship and involvement of pupils within it. Invite faith leaders into worship so they fully understand the spiritual significance and pattern of each element.

Consistency and integrity—Be clear and consistent about what will and will not happen in worship. They need to be able to trust that the experience of worship and school life will be as has been described.

Do not assume that what one family believes is what all the families think. Keep asking questions and learn about the communities represented in the school.

In summary, deep-rooted, trusting relationships with parents and the wider community are key. In time, this will cultivate opportunities for open dialogue where truths can be shared and robust conversations are welcomed. These conversations should not be left to chance, so must be carefully planned and thought through. This will prevent misunderstandings or hurt being caused.

Questions to Consider

- How might this wisdom strengthen collective worship in your context?
- How might an understanding of one another deepen the spiritual flourishing of all?

Flourishing Spiritually

The SIAMS 2023 Framework asks school leaders, 'How is collective worship enabling pupils and adults to flourish spiritually?' But what does this mean?

Sally Burns and Georgeanne Lamont's description brings clarity and colour to a concept that is sometimes misunderstood:

> Spirituality is a source of creativity open to us all. It brings that quality of aliveness which sparks inquiry, ideas, observations, insights, empathy, artistic expression, earnest endeavour and playfulness. It opens us to life and to each other. Spirituality is a thread which runs through our life, bringing hope, compassion, thankfulness, courage, peace and a sense of purpose and meaning to everyday, while reaching beyond the immediate world of the visible and tangible. It drives us to seek and stay true to values not ruled by material success.[18]

This description of spirituality paints a picture of what spiritual flourishing through collective worship might look like. This articulation is not tied to a particular faith but seeks to demonstrate the impact that both exploring spirituality and being spiritual can have. The list of qualities Burns and Lamont set out is brought to life through rich spiritual interactions in worship and everyday school experiences. When pupils are given the reins and learn how to lead others in worship, these qualities are exemplified and embodied. Therefore, how might empowering pupils to take the lead in worship contribute to the spiritual flourishing of individual pupils and the wider community?

A Shared Spiritual Language

Spiritual practices vary greatly across different cultures and religions. One of the most universal is prayer. Whilst the words, posture or recipient of the prayer may differ, the desire to join in a spiritual communion with the divine connects believers. Therefore, by recognizing shared beliefs and intentions, prayer unites—even when participants are praying in their own distinct faith traditions.

Ruth Braunstein explained from a sociological perspective, that, 'Prayer is a practice that can help people from different religions find a shared identity by coming together.'[19] Charles Spurgeon was quoted as saying, 'True prayer is neither a mere mental exercise nor a vocal performance. It is far deeper than that—it is spiritual transaction with the creator of heaven and earth.'[20] This articulation describes prayer as an act that goes above the physical to unite the human and divine.

Questions to Consider

- How does prayer unite your community during worship?
- Does it contribute to the spiritual flourishing of all?

> During worship, all our children are invited to pray. Our prayers all come from the Christian tradition. However, when I lead the prayers, I always start it with 'Dear God,' since for me, as a Muslim, this connects what I am praying to Allah. Some of our Muslim children choose to close their prayers with '*Amyin*' (which is Arabic for amen), while others say 'Amen' and others will bow their head out of respect. Each term we hold a prayer event where the whole school community is invited to pray for our school, country and world. As we prayed for peace in the Middle East, prayers in Arabic, Bengali, Hebrew and English were uttered from both adults and children. This was a powerful spiritual moment for us as we united together in praying for peace, using our shared language of prayer.
>
> Assistant head teacher, Church of England primary school

I would be naive to suggest that creating authentic acts of Christian worship in a diverse community is always plain sailing. Issues and concerns will arise and need to be navigated carefully. In the Grove booklet, *Nurturing Healthy Diversity in Church Schools,* the authors detail four church schools in Birmingham that serve diverse communities (social, ethnic, economic and religious).[21] The detailed stories and practical wisdom therein offers support for leaders to consider how they can accommodate and celebrate difference and diversity successfully.

4 Gennesaret—A Cultivated Land of Fertile Soil

In ancient times, the fertility of the soil, temperate climate, geographical location and well-drained and irrigated soil created the perfect conditions for abundant growth at Gennesaret. Ultimately, without these conditions working together, the variety of trees and plants would not have flourished. Before pupil leaders can thrive, the culture of the school or 'soil' must be conducive to growth. A culture built on the principles of grace, trust, acceptance, patience and courage will support pupil leaders to flourish and grow authentically.

I have the privilege of joining in with acts of worship in many different schools. It is always a joy to see how creative both adult and pupil leaders are when it comes to planning and leading acts of worship.

The principles outlined below have come from my own reflections, having led, observed and discussed hundreds of acts of worship. When a school culture is built on these principles, young people will want to be an active part of worship because they know their voices are valued and trusted.

Cultivating the Soil—Principles that Promote Growth and Flourishing

Grace

Grace—'the willingness to be fair and to forgive.'

Things will go wrong! Grace involves:

- Giving the young people space to try and try again;
- Loving them enough not to comment negatively, tut or sigh when they stumble over words or forget to say something;
- Being understanding when the plan is not clear enough or the message gets slightly muddled;
- Providing repeated opportunities to try things out and discover for themselves what works and what does not;
- Everyone knowing it is OK when worship led by pupils feels or looks different to what is 'normal';

- Forgiveness of each other and themselves, when they feel the act of worship did not go to plan.

> When our pupils first began leading worship, they found delivering their message a challenge. They often stumbled over their words, spoke too quietly and hesitated when responding to questions and comments from other pupils. Over time, the pupils became more confident in themselves and what they were delivering. Our school culture of grace and forgiveness meant that mistakes were seen as learning. As a collective, we encouraged, supported and gave them space to try again and again.
>
> Collective worship leader, Church of England primary school

Trust

Trust—to have confidence in something, or to believe in someone.

Young people grow and develop best within relationships built on trust. When teachers say, 'We trust you to lead our school community in worship,' or, 'We trust what you have to say to us and that you have considered carefully the message for today,' it is a huge honour for young people and their self-worth and confidence grows as a result.

> As a pupil worship leader I feel that what I have to say is valued by the adults in the school, otherwise they wouldn't have asked us to lead them in worship. There were times when I didn't feel like I knew what to say. Our teacher encouraged us to spend time thinking about the story again and trust ourselves that we would find the key message to share with others within it.
>
> Pupil worship leader, Year 6

Patience

Patience—the ability to wait, or to continue doing something despite difficulties, without complaining or becoming annoyed.

Planning and leading acts of worship will not always be perfect the first time around. Young people need time to expand their experience, develop their delivery style and their ability to respond to reflections from those listening. Therefore, the school community must remain patient with those leading.

Young people will need reminding sensitively that it takes time to develop the skills needed to lead worship. All too often, they want to see improvements and perfection straight away. Teaching them to persevere and be patient is a crucial part of the process: 'But if we hope for what we do not see, we wait for it with patience' (Rom 8.25; NRSV). Working with a group of young people to plan and lead acts of worship will take forbearance. A huge amount of time and commitment will be needed by all those involved. As a very wise teacher I once worked with used to say, 'Be kind to yourself': you cannot expect everything to get sorted overnight.

Courage

Courage—to be brave and confident enough to do what you believe in.

For pupil worship leaders to step up and lead worship, they need to feel secure. They need to know that their mistakes will be supported, their nervousness will be understood and it is safe to take risks. This takes a huge amount of courage from the young leaders, especially when they are leading worship in front of their peers. The adults involved also need to be brave in letting go and creating space for the young people to lead in their way and style. Pupil-led worship can be messy! It will look different from adult-led worship. Collective worship is not meant to be a performance, but a moment in time that leaves you changed. It is a time to breathe and space for all to grow spiritually. Once a school community understands this and embraces the variety and colour young people bring, worship will be enhanced and spiritually deeper for it.

Curiosity

Curiosity—the desire to learn or find out about people or something.

Schools are rich places of questioning and curiosity. Most cultivate the joy of enquiry and inquisitiveness through well-planned encounters and experiences. Lessons encourage pupils to ask, and respond to, bold and visionary questions. Therefore draw upon these attributes and allow pupils to be curious and question what they see around them. Use these questions and views to inspire the acts of worship they plan. Encouraging a culture where pupils and adults can ask challenging questions and have the space to ponder, will deepen the worship experience for all:

> It can be uncomfortable to allow young people to create meaning, but this is where they internalize learning, where it becomes their own.[22]

Young people want to explore what is going on, usually starting a conversation with 'why' or 'why not.' Use this natural curiosity to gather their opinion of worship, by opening an intentional dialogue about why things happen. I am sure this will bring challenge to those leading, but a fresh viewpoint is always a good thing.

Acceptance

Acceptance—willingness of people to believe in a new idea or to include all.

All young people need to know they are welcome to be a worship leader, including those from all faiths and none. As we explored in chapter two, all voices should be heard, as all bring something unique to the group. It is important to note that being a worship leader does not mean you have to be a confident, up-front speaker. The worship leadership team should take on many roles. Some young people will want to be part of the planning team but will not want a speaking role. Others may enjoy welcoming the school community into worship or being responsible for putting the PowerPoint presentation together and operating the technology. An effective pupil worship leadership team will accept and embrace all.

Those who volunteer to be pupil leaders of worship will reflect the demographic of your school. Therefore, if your school serves a diverse faith community, your pupil worship leaders will be representative of this.

> I am a worship leader in my church school, and I come from a Muslim family. We plan and lead worship regularly for our school community, with each of us taking an active role in the planning and delivery of worship. When leading worship, I show a deep respect for the Christian faith and the messages shared from the Bible. However, this is not my belief. When we pray, I pray to Allah. I know what the *Quran* teaches me about living a good life and I draw on this during the reflection time. This passage helps me to understand this.
>
> > 'I do not serve that which you serve,
> > Nor do you serve him whom I serve:
> > You shall have your religion and I shall have my religion.'[23]
>
> I am taught to show deep respect for the beliefs of my school friends. I try and live this out every day, especially in my important worship leader role.
>
> Pupil worship leader, Year 6

In summary, creating a rich, safe worshipping community takes time. Creating a space, where all flourish spiritually, whether they are leading, serving or joining for worship, takes genuine investment from the whole school community. The impact of the fertile soil and climate in Gennesaret enabled diverse trees to grow and thrive. In the same way, for pupils to grow and develop as leaders of worship, the right conditions and culture need to be in place. How 'fertile is your school soil'?

5

The What and the How

In order to set off on the journey of gathering and training pupils to be worship leaders, two fundamental foundations need to be in place before any practicalities can be considered.

First, are you really clear about your 'why'? Reflecting on your thinking from chapter two, *why* do you want to train up a group of pupil worship leaders? What might this look like for you? The role and place of pupil worship leaders will look different in every school context, so be driven by *your* why, not what the school down the road does!

Secondly, consider the principles and example of Gennesaret in chapters three and four. Is your school community prepared and committed to welcoming and empowering pupil worship leaders? How can you ensure that all members of the community are fully behind this group, so they can grow and flourish in their role?

Once you have a clear 'why,' the 'how' and 'what' will flow naturally from this.

Why Do You Want to Be a Pupil Worship Leader?

- 'To act as a role model for the younger children'
- 'To teach children and adults in my school about our Christian values'
- 'So I can share Bible stories with other children'
- 'I thought it would be fun'
- 'It gives me an opportunity to develop my confidence in speaking in front of people'
- 'To share something of Jesus with other children'
- 'So I could grow as a leader'
- 'I like helping out, so I knew I could do plenty of this in this role'
- 'It's a great opportunity to try something new'
- 'So I can share my thinking and ideas with the whole school'

- 'I knew it would be something I would enjoy, and I do!'

Pupils from various church schools

What

When discussing pupils leading worship with a group of collective worship leaders, I challenged them to consider what this might mean. The teachers described times when pupils regularly led sections within the act of worship. However, when we drilled into this, they shared that pupils were either given a script written by an adult to read or led the opening and closing liturgical phrases. From this discussion it was clear that whilst the voice of the child was being heard, their own inner thinking and reflections were not.

This conversation set me off on another trail of enquiry. How could the internal thoughts, ideas and reflections of pupils feature regularly in worship? Could they be fully included in each step of the planning and evaluation of collective worship with decreasing adult intervention?

The 2021–2022 SIAMS Annual Report states:

> It is obvious how pupil leadership of worship could make a positive contribution to individuals' spiritual development and to the spiritual flourishing of the whole school community.[24]

It is not just me who thinks having pupil worship leaders is a positive idea!

In this chapter I will share two models for including the voice of children regularly within worship. The first model has been used successfully by leaders to give pupil leaders the tools to plan an entire act of worship. The second model, which is explained through a case study, demonstrates how one school includes the voice of pupils in every act of worship. Both have a place in the worshipping life of a school. Always be guided by your 'why' when considering how you will include the voice of pupils within your worship.

Model One—Planning an Entire Act of Worship

This planning model draws its inspiration from the monastic practice *lectio divina*, or divine reading. It simply asks the pupils to read and reflect on a biblical passage a number of times, before sharing their reflections with each other. As the pupils listen, reflect and share with each other, the key message from the Scripture will emerge. The pupils then use this message to shape the act of worship.

- Gather the pupils together. Invite them to be still and quiet before beginning the process.

a) Share the Bible story or passage. Choose one person to read it out loud, with the others following.

b) Think and ponder on it silently—what ideas and thoughts jump out? Invite the pupils to annotate or highlight the Bible passage with these thoughts as they listen.

c) Share any thoughts: 'I wonder what jumped out at you which words or phrases stood out?' Give space and time for all to contribute to this if they wish.

- Repeat steps a-c twice more, with a different voice reading the passage each time.
- Gather all the thoughts and ideas together: 'Having listened really carefully, what do we think the message of this Bible passage is?'

This model does not expect those present to believe in the biblical passage being read and explored. It simply asks pupils to listen carefully and draw out the key message.

Once the key message has been decided, support the pupils in planning the act of worship using the school pattern and structure. The following questions will support pupils in ensuring they have thought through all the elements:

- From our discussions, what is the key message we want to share with the school family?
- How will we gather our school family?
- How will we read / teach / illustrate the Bible story / passage?
- How will we reflect and think about the Bible story / passage?
- How will we pray together?
- What will we sing and when?
- How will we send our school family out from worship?

Then decide together who will lead and take responsibility for each part.

We have been using this model for a while now to give a structure to our planning meetings. Over the course of the year, our pupil worship leaders have become more confident in speaking up and sharing what they have drawn out from the Bible text. They are often amazed at what they hear through reading the Bible text a number of times.

At times, the pupils disagree about how the message should be delivered or who should lead each part. Part of our worship leader training focuses in on disagreeing well and how to handle situations when you can't agree on a way forward.

Collective worship leader, Church of England primary school

Our inward culture of acceptance, love and compassion means that all our pupils, not just the worship leaders, feel safe to share their thinking without fear of being judged or laughed at. Therefore, when things do go wrong—forgotten lines, stumbled words, a muddled message or clumsy response to a child's answer—no one reacts, they just wait in a supportive silence until it gets sorted or gets back on track. Reflection and evaluation form a central part of our worship leader meetings, so when moments like this arise, we discuss and work through them together. We share our feelings, consider how we could improve things next time and celebrate what went well together. This helps us to shape future acts of worship.

Collective worship leader, Church of England secondary school

Worship, Not a Performance

It is important to remember, collective worship is not a performance. A perfectly polished worship presentation may not allow space for spiritual reflection or interaction with those present. There is a myth that if the children are leading worship, we should expect a performance that has been practised and practised. This is not the reality of school life. Do we expect the adults leading to be perfectly polished and deserving of a clap after they have spoken? Hopefully not. There clearly is a balance to be had between an act of worship that is worshipful and an act of worship performance.

For Christians, worship is a time to honour God, giving their best out of gratitude for all that has been given to them. Therefore, worship should be planned and led well, so as to give glory to God. Christians are encouraged to bring themselves as they are to worship. In the same way, we should expect anyone who is leading worship to come as they are. Prepare and consider carefully what needs to be shared, but do not perform the life out of it.

However, for worship to be heard and have an impact, pupils need to be taught to speak clearly, to deliver their message confidently and know how to respond to answers given by other pupils. So spend time with the pupils developing their voice and delivery, rather than practising a performance. This will help your pupils feel confident and empowered to share what they have planned.

Model Two—Pupil Worship Leaders Every Day

The second model is a more organic one, where the voice of pupil leaders is encouraged, shared and heard each day.

Flowing from our distinctive Christian vision, the inclusion of all voices, especially those of children, is a key part of who we are. As a leadership team we reflected on the purpose and role of pupil worship leaders in our school, as we felt their voice was regularly missing from worship. Traditionally, the pupil worship leaders would gather each term to plan and lead an entire act of worship. At times this felt like a performance, with the focus often being on the children, not the biblical message or act of worship itself. So we wanted to move away from this model, to create a safe space where the voice of the pupil leaders was welcomed and valued as much as the adults leading. By doing this, the pupils have become an integral part of the daily worshipping life of the school.

Working in small teams on a weekly rota, our Year 6 worship leaders take it in turns to serve whoever is leading, whether in the school or church. When questions are posed and opportunities offered to discuss the Bible verse or message, the pupil leaders move amongst the other children, listening to their responses and reflections. They then feed back to the school community all that they have heard, plus their own thoughts. Their articulation and summary of the message is often clearer and more child friendly, which helps the rest of the school connect with, and reflect on, the message for their own lives.

Pupil worship leaders regularly share of themselves through prayer. Following some initial guidance, they draw upon what they have heard to create spontaneous, heartfelt prayers. At times, their ability to navigate difficult situations or capture the feelings of the school community through prayer is profound. Their simple, uncomplicated voice often stirs emotions, bringing a tangibly deeper spiritual connection between us and God. This prayerful freedom has inspired other pupils to pray with confidence. It also gives deeper connection to all that has been discussed.

Those leading worship fully rely on the pupil worship leaders to capture, and be the voice of, the school. Acting as the eyes on the ground, they bring wise reflection and insight which helps to shape and develop worship further.

For us, growing pupil worship leaders to be an integral part of daily worship is essential. Without them, we would miss out on hearing their rich wisdom and simple, yet profound, insights. We have grown spiritually because of them. Our pupil worship leaders are confident and joyful because they know that their insights and regular input is valued and cherished by the whole school community.

Collective worship leader, Church of England primary school

How

Now to the practicalities. As the two models have emphasized, for pupils to grow as leaders they need to be heard and valued in this role. Therefore, be realistic when starting a group, so that times and dates are manageable with everything else going on each week. Create a pattern and plan for your context and community that is sustainable.

Questions to Consider

- Who will run the group and work with the pupil worship leaders? Look wider into your community, as it does not have to be a teacher or the head teacher. Who is the best person to nurture your growing leaders?
- When and how often will they meet? How many sessions will the pupils need in order to put together their act of worship?
- How often will the pupils take the responsibility for leading worship? Be realistic.
- Which pupils might be involved? Schools manage this in many different ways. Whoever you choose, it should be inclusive of all, reflecting the community your school serves.
- How will they become worship leaders? Do they volunteer, get nominated or write a letter to show their commitment to the role?
- What training will you put in place to support your worship leaders in understanding their role in worship and within school?[25]
- How will the school community know that these pupils are worship leaders? Could you put together a commissioning service where the children are given something to wear as an outward sign of this role?

Empowering pupils to take the lead takes time and significant investment by the adults leading them. However, as explored in chapter two, if we genuinely want to hear the voice of children, the time spent listening and guiding them is of immeasurable worth.

6 Tending Your School like Gennesaret

I hope you have caught my 'why' and developed your own reasons for why the voice of young people should be heard and included regularly in worship. Having ambition that it is possible is a great place to start.

Throughout this book I have drawn upon the analogy of the fertile soil once found in Gennesaret to illustrate how, if the soil and climate of your school is right, collective worship can both bring—and give—life to all. However, for the trees and plants to produce crops or flourish alongside each other, there must be constant tending of the soil and monitoring of conditions, otherwise the plants will not thrive or continue to grow.

In chapter three, we explored the importance of investing in relationships with faith groups to ensure worship is truly inclusive of all. The shared anecdotes illustrate where this has been done well, ensuring pupils of all faiths are included within, and are part of, worship. However, where differences are not explored in open and honest conversations, disagreements and negative feelings can take hold. This could result in a school community where not all are able to flourish alongside each other in worship. What impact might this have on the school community and the spiritual flourishing of all?

Freedom and security within a school community is key. Freedom to live out your faith or beliefs knowing they will be celebrated and embraced. Security for pupils and the wider community that worship will be truly inclusive.

We also have this shared hope, that the hidden treasures within our pupils will cultivate a fertile soil and beauty within worship. Growing and developing confident and spiritual pupil leaders of worship cannot be left to chance. It will take constant nurturing and investment in the school culture, community and pupils themselves. This will take time and we will probably never know the true value or lifelong impact on the pupil or wider community:

> Children are more likely to flourish if their voices are regularly heard, truly valued and acted upon, not as employees of the future but as leaders in the present.[26]

What a gift for a young person to know that their voice, insights and spiritual awareness is cherished and valued. What impact might this confidence and belief in them have on their future?

I hope that, through this booklet, you have been inspired to ensure that the voice of pupils, as spiritual agents, is regularly heard within worship. I also hope you feel empowered to hand over the reins to young people to plan and lead worship as equal partners.

> Imagine if collective worship was an experience children relished.
>
> Imagine if they felt as special in this sacred space as the children who stepped through the wardrobe into Narnia.
>
> Imagine if they felt trusted enough to share their insights, their ideas and individuality.[27]

Notes

1 R Coles, *The Spiritual Life of Children* (Boston, MI: Houghton Mifflin, 1990).

2 Department of Education Office, *Religious Education and Collective Worship Circular* 1/94 (1994), paragraphs 50, 57.

3 Church of England Education Office, *Guidance for Collective Worship* (London: Archbishops' Council, 2021) p 1.

4 M James, Church of England Education Office, 'The Annual Report of the National Director of the Statutory Inspection of Anglican and Methodist Schools 2022-23' (churchofengland.org) p 3.

5 A K M Pang, 'Prophetic Wonder with Children in the Call to Teach,' in E DeGaynor (ed), *Let the Children Lead: Exploring Children's Spirituality Today* (Alexandria, VA: VTS Press, 2023) p 21.

6 K Rahner, 'Ideas for a Theology of Childhood' in *Theological Investigations, Volume 8: Further Theology of the Spiritual Life* (1963), quoted in E DeGaynor, *Let the Children Lead, op cit,* p 24.

7 D Hay, R Nye, *Children's Spirituality* (London: Church House Publishing, 2009) p 6.

8 R Goldman, *Religious Thinking from Childhood to Adolescence* (London: Routledge and Kegan Paul, 1964) p 14, quoted in D Hay and R Nye, *The Spirit of the Child* (London: Harper Collins, 1998) p 50.

9 D Hay with R Nye, *The Spirit of the Child, op cit,* p 50.

10 D Oswell, 'The Agency of Children: From family to global human rights' (2013), p 270, cited in A K M Pang, *op cit,* p 24.

11 A K M Pang in E DeGaynor, *Let the Children Lead, op cit.*

12 M Chater, *Jesus Christ, Learner Teacher* (London: SCM Press, 2020) p 6.

13 *ibid,* p 6.

14 T Cooling, preface to A Casson, S Hulbert, M Woolley and R Bowie, *Faith in the Nexus Report* (Canterbury: NICER, Canterbury Christ Church University, 2020) p 4.

15 S Chalke, J Rowe, *Different Podcast—Episode 2* (Oasis Podcasts, 2023).

16 R Nye, *Children's Spirituality, op cit,* p 34.

17 Church of England Education Office, *Our Hope for a Flourishing Future* (London: CEFEL, 2023) p 9.

18 S Burns, G Lamont, *Values and Visions* (London: Hodder and Stoughton, 1995).

19 R Braunstein, 'When Can Religion Help Bridge Our Differences?' in *Greater Good Magazine* (Berkeley, CA: University of California, 2024).

20 Taken from Spurgeon's sermon, 'The Throne of Grace,' preached in 1871. Transcript: https://www.spurgeon.org/resource-library/sermons/the-throne-of-grace/#flipbook/

21 D Whisker, L Vickerage-Goddard and S Phihlaja , *Nurturing Healthy Diversity in Church Schools* (Grove Education booklet eD 44). This builds on P French, *Church Schools in a Multi-faith Community* (Grove Education booklet eD4).

22 M L Larson, 'Does the church care if children can think?' in M I Larson and R J Keeley (eds), *Bridging Theory and Practice in Children's Spirituality* (Grand Rapids, MI: Zondervan, 2020) p 197.

23 *Quran,* Surah 109, 1–6.

24 M James, Church of England Education Office, 'The Annual Report of the National Director of the Statutory Inspection of Anglican and Methodist Schools 2021–22' (churchofengland.org) p 11.

25 R Swansbury, *Where can I go for practical help?* A book and resource pack to support school leaders in training worship leaders is available to purchase and download: https://www.cpo.org.uk/c-of-e-print-shop/other-cofe-initiatives/cofe-diocese/diocese-of-canterbury.html (2019).

26 Church of England Education Office, *Our Hope for a Flourishing Future, op cit,* p 9.

27 Paraphrased from B Farrell, quoted in J McCann, *Spiritual Garments* (Brandon, Suffolk: Decani Books, 2006) p 7.